Courtney Mulholland, a poet from Northern Ireland, has struggled with her mental health, trauma and sexuality on and off over the years, but finally found solace in reading and the worlds hidden inside books. Courtney finally decided to put pen to paper and write about her feelings and experiences, in order to share them with the world, and if possible, help some people feel less alone.

Bottles of orange whiskey, manic episodes, sad songs, and female rage, every time I dreamt of being in another world, lost myself in daydreams and found myself in books.

The love notes I never received, the texts I never sent, every word I never said, every ghost story, and every regret, the nights I cried myself to sleep, and the mornings I woke up smiling.

– ***CM***

Courtney Mulholland

Ghost Stories & Love Notes

Austin Macauley Publishers®
London * Cambridge * New York * Sharjah

A CIP catalogue record for this title is available from the British Library.

ISBN 9781035875801 (Paperback)
ISBN 9781035875818 (ePub e-book)

www.austinmacauley.com

First Published 2025
Austin Macauley Publishers Ltd®
1 Canada Square
Canary Wharf
London
E14 5AA

This book is for me, from me, but I still have some people to thank for their unconditional support throughout my life and my writing.

My mum, Lesley Mulholland, for not only being my mother, but for being my best friend, my safe place to land, and my greatest support, who not only gave me my voice but showed me how to use it.

My dad, Dinky Mulholland, the first man I ever loved; thank you for showing me how to be strong, for always picking me up every time I fell, for always keeping me safe, no matter what life threw at me.

My Nanny, for being my pillar of constant, unflinching and unmoving love, throughout my life.

A love letter to the girl I used to be.

You are glorious and spectacular
you are fierce, brave, and strong,
my darling, you are perfect in every way
never let anyone tell you otherwise.
You are, exactly who you are meant to be
nothing and no one can take that from you.

You are everything you were born to be
even if you don't know it yet
my darling, you have a remarkable kind of magic
flowing within you, even if you can't feel it.
That magic is yours, and yours alone
no one can dull it, or steal it.

You are glorious and spectacular
you are fierce, and brave, and strong
but most importantly, you are loved.
My darling, you are so beloved
never doubt it.

– ***CM***

Dear everyone with a broken heart.

Get drunk on your favourite drink.
Dance on as many tables as you can
until your legs give out.
Kiss some strangers you'll never see again and cry.
Cry until you run out of tears.

But no matter how broken your heart is, do not beg.
Never beg for them to come back
because you are worth so much
more than you could possibly know.

– CM

As life twists and turns
and it changes around us
we can’t always twist and change with it
but we do lose. Maybe we lose someone
or we lose a piece of ourselves
but, the world keeps spinning
never slowing down.

Life keeps coming at us
around and around and around
the world goes on.
No matter what the world
throws at us we’ll always find a way
to build ourselves up
bigger and better than before.

By losing something
by losing everything
every so often, we manage to win.
We win at making ourselves better
better versions than we were before.

We are the generation
that has perfected the art
of making losing look like winning
and making a winning situation
out of every game, we lose.

– CM

'You are in a cage.'

Maybe that's the point.
I locked myself in a cage
that I constructed for myself
without a key to freedom.
I have no way out
and I have nowhere to run
I am locked inside my past
like an anchor, weighing me down
to the darkest depths of my mind.
The price for my freedom has never been higher
but, it's a price I'm willing to pay.

I built that cage
I will tear it down.

You are in a cage.

'No, you are.'

– CM

Fuck.

What am I supposed to feel?
Should I be upset?
When they call me R-rated
it's not their fault they don't understand
what it's like to be me.

They are all so busy
looking for angels
to save them
from themselves
but, I'm seeking the devil
for a bit of truth and honesty.

I'm done seeing the world
through rose-coloured glasses
I got over searching for angels
because I'm already free.

Even if I am a little R-rated
maybe even strictly PG-13
but in the end
everyone is just like me.
A little messed up and slightly damaged.

We're all freaks
except you're looking for angels

and I've already settled for the devil.

– CM

I think, deep down
I've always had a thing for the villains
the ones that I see on TV or in movies
I always seem to fall for the bad guys
the ones that I read about
in all, my favourite books.

I guess, I've always been in my villain era.

– CM

I think I made you up inside my head
so that I wouldn't get too lonely
whenever everybody else left me behind
I built myself a house made of paper
from the pages of every book I've read.
That way I'd always have a place
where I'd never have to be alone
but every time I look around
there's only me.

I think I made you up inside my head
so that I wouldn't get too sad
when I spent all my time in my mind
instead, I'll spend my days with you
telling you every story I know.
Just me and you and my paper house.

– ***CM***

I don’t know how to be okay
without harming myself
and those words feel like acid
as they drip from my tongue
because I don’t understand
how something so harmful
could make me feel so much better.
I don’t know how to be okay
without seeing my blood
dripping from my veins
like a waterfall of my DNA
because it reminds me I’m alive.
Maybe someone can teach me
how to be okay.

But, out of everything
I don’t know how to be okay
with being saved
because I’m not really sure if I deserve it
and I don’t know how to appreciate it.

– CM

I'll go through the motions
back and forth over, and over again
living is as easy as brushing my teeth.

But it's nothing like brushing my teeth
it doesn't last the length of time
it takes to sing Happy Birthday twice
and I can't wash the bad parts down the drain
mistakes aren't that easy to wash away.

I used to think most things were easy
that everything was simple
just like brushing my teeth
but then brushing my teeth
became a daily struggle.

Back and forth
and back and forth
singing happy birthday
in my head on repeat
over and over again
as difficult as brushing my teeth.

– CM

Ask me the stuff that is important
I dare you.
Stop long enough to ask me
the stuff that really matters

My favourite:
author
actor
musician
and artist
but you should know
my answer will always remain the same.

My answer will always be:
all of them
everyone who has ever tried
and everyone who hasn't yet.

– CM

I know that most people
A lot of people
will never understand
why goodbye is my favourite word
in every language.

But, no one else needs too
none of it really matters
to anybody else but me
my memories hold my reasons

No one will ever know why
I find goodbyes the sweetest
but my memories hold the truth
and that’s enough for me.

– ***CM***

Twenty reasons why I am terrified of my sexuality.

1. The lack of acknowledgement that surrounded me in school.
2. The idea of having to come out over and over again for my entire life.
3. The overwhelming feeling of not fitting in.
4. The high chances of losing everyone I love.
5. The damage to my mental health when I tried to convince myself I was straight.
6. The fear of invalidating any feelings I had for someone because they don't fit my sexuality.
7. Always having to deal with the questions of how long I've known and how I knew.
8. The idea of losing parts of who I am because people will only refer to me as my sexuality.
9. Being aware that people will hate me without knowing anything else about me.
10. Knowing that I will be someone's token queer in their life.
11. Knowing that my life will be used as a story people share when they talk about equality.
12. Feeling like I'm invalidating my sexuality because I do not match the stereotypes of how I should act or how I should be.
13. I will be used as proof that someone is not homophobic because I'm in their life.
14. Having to explain why I am in love with a woman, yet I still fall for male fictional characters.
15. Knowing that some people will never admit that my 'phase' was never actually a phase.
16. Having people who barely know me tell me that I am just confused and that I haven't found the right man yet.
17. At 16 years old, when I finally found the courage to come out, people assumed it was because a boy rejected me.
18. If I meet someone new, and I tell them I am queer, I never know how they will react.
19. If I tell people I am queer, they begin to poke holes in my sexual assault story, by questioning why I was with a boy to begin with.
20. Because it's the twenty-first century, yet being a member of the LGBTQ+ still puts a target on your back, and I am sick of running.

– CM

It's 2:10 am
and I am reorganising my 200+
books onto a total of 12 shelves
because my brain won't let me sleep
because when I'm awake
is the only time it can torment me.
My head keeps me awake
so that my memories can torture me
and keep me locked up
inside my own personal prison.

At 6:02 am
I am surrounded by darkness
and I am trying my hardest
not to cave into it.
I have become a monster
that my mind created
corrupted by the voices
that scream inside my head.
They are driving me over the edge
but then again
I've always been comfortable in chaos
because I've found a way
to make the depths of hell feel like home.

The darkness inside me
forged my mind into a weapon
that someday
I will use it to destroy myself.
My demons were not born
they were created
and it's time for them
to meet their maker.

– CM

Sometimes
I want to vanish into the night sky
and become nothing more than
a whisper on the wind.
I want people to forget me
in every way possible
I want every memory of me
to fade from this world
until I am nothing more than
a ghost dancing alone.

I would like to vanish
I would like to be forgotten
because I'm not afraid of dying
but I am terrified of living.
So, when it's 10 pm
and I'm staring into
an open flame in front of me
it occurs to me that maybe
being forgotten by everyone
isn't the worst idea I've ever had.

– CM

I'm glad I never told you
how much I love to write
in the year we were together
it was the one thing I kept to myself
while you knew everything else about me.

If you had known
you would have found a way
to weave yourself
around my work
until you were suffocating my words.

I'm glad I never told you
how much I love to write
because I would have felt bad
not writing anything about
you but you never gave me anything
worth writing about.

If I showed you the way
words poured from my mind
into something much more magical
I know you would have found a way
to make me feel like it wasn't magic at all.

I'm glad I never told you
how much I love to write
because all it would have taken was
for you to have told me
that no one was listening
and you would have
silenced my voice forever.

I'm glad I never told you
how much I love to write
because it's the one piece of me
I would have never got back
if you had taken it away.

– CM

I want to be known as
a Final Girl.
It sounds a lot more
poetic than being called
‘a survivor’.

A Final Girl is more than just
the one who survives
the Final Girl is the one
who paid in blood to reach the end
the only one who manages to kill the thing
trying to kill her.

If being a Final Girl isn’t something to strive for
then I don’t know what is.

– ***CM***

The truth is just because I'm clean
that doesn't mean I don't miss it
I miss it more than I should
more than I ever thought I could
I guess that is just a part of being addicted
even to an inanimate object
or a feeling.
I think I'll always miss it
I'll always miss something about it.

Maybe the way it made me feel
or the way it reminded me
that I was alive, or maybe
I'll miss the subtle way it
silenced the world.

– ***CM***

The blinding truth is
that I am my father's daughter
I am his flesh
I am his blood
and I have his temper
I am the best of him
and I am the worst.

I am my father's flesh and blood
I am made of everything
that makes him who he is.
I am made of so much of him
that people tell me
I look just like him.
From the freckles on my face
to the natural colour of my hair
and, most importantly, my eyes
I have my father's eyes.

I am my father's daughter
and nothing could stop me
from being proud of it.
I am proud to be his daughter
because I know my father
I know his heart and soul
I know his happiness and his sadness
I know his pain and his every strength
because I am made of every piece of him.

I am my father's daughter
and that means I have nothing to fear
I have nothing to hide
and I have nothing to prove to anyone.

– CM

You know what they say about hope?
That a little goes a long way?
No. That it breeds eternal misery.

I used to believe that
hope was a beautiful thing
in fact; I was besotted
with the idea of hope
and everything it could bring.

Every day was better
everything seemed golden
and brand new
and I put life on a pedestal
but, I got distracted
and I got blinded.

The rose-coloured glasses
broke and shattered
the golden light
turned into flames
the pedestal I put life on
crashed and burnt.

I caught my reflection
in a cracked mirror,
and it was like a landslide
pulling me down to
what I was used to
before I became besotted
with a four-letter word.

Hope: A little goes a long way.

Hope: It breeds eternal misery.

– CM

My pain should not have lasted for an eternity
and in my heart and my head
I know that it didn't
but it felt like forever
within a number of years.
Within that eternity
my pain became a succubus
that has consumed
my entire body
and is now picking
my soul from its teeth
with my very own bones
savouring every moment.
To everyone else
my pain lasted but a moment
to me, it had been an eternity.
A lifetime worth of pain
within twenty-something years.
Stuck in a never-ending battle
with the voices in my head
that I'm pretty sure were trying to kill me.

It has not been forever
but for me, it has been an eternity.

– CM

We have bigger regrets
to live with than
the things we tattooed
on our precious porcelain skin.

– CM

I will ask you if you love me
one hundred times a day
for the rest of forever
until I feel as if you're telling me the truth
and, the brutal part is
it won't feel like the truth
until you finally say

'No. I don't'

– CM

I am magic I say
as I look at myself
in the bathroom mirror
tears drying on my cheeks
my lips bitten and bleeding
from holding in my cries.

I am magic I say
as I wrap myself
in a hoodie three sizes too big
and the same sweatpants
I've been wearing
for a week, in and out of bed.

I am magic I say
as I get back into bed
and put on the same show
I've watched seven times
and cry at the sad parts, all over again.

I am magic I say
as I coat myself in sadness
allowing it to take over
and turn everything golden
into something dark.

I am magic I say
as I take a shower and wash my hair
while I brush my teeth
and change my clothes
in over a week
and I finally start to feel good.

I am magic I say
to remind myself
I made of some kind of magic
and I will always stay golden
no matter what life throws at me.

– CM

I know you'll love me
when the blissful beginning is over
when the honeymoon phase is gone
and the shine has worn off
and we have no more firsts.
I know you'll love me
when we fight
and when we don't
when I call you names
and insult your music taste.
I know you'll love me
when I'm happy
and even more when I'm not
when every piece of me is broken
or, when I'm all glued back together.
I know you will love me
not because of how you look at me
when I'm dancing, smiling, or singing.
Not because of how you look at
me when I'm all dressed up
with my makeup done.

I know you will love me
because of how you look at me
when I'm sad
when I'm curled up in bed and crying
because of how you look at me
when I've been beaten down by the world
and I feel like giving up.
That is how I know you will love
simply for me.

– CM

I am a fool
because I loved you all
and I lost you one by one.
It felt like pieces of my heart
falling around me
just like snow or confetti.
I am the one
who pushed you all
as far away from me
and my mess as I could
until you all let go.

I am a fool
because I want you all
to be a part of my life forever
but I gave you no choice
and I left no other options
but for you to pull the ripcord
that bound us all together.
I loved you all
with every part of my being
and every fibre of my soul
and I was destroying us
like the snake destroyed Eden.

I am a fool
because I chose this
I chose to lose you all
rather than taking the risk
of breaking your hearts
for the rest of my life.
You loved me
just like I loved you
I just wasn't worth it
not in the end.

– CM

I exist to be a body
to take up space
and fill in the gaps.
I exist to be
the punchline of the joke
and the funny fat friend in the story.
I exist to be the anti-hero
and the morally grey character
who will always come up with a lie
when the truth isn't good enough.

I exist to be nothing more than a body
to take the beating
the scars and the bruises
and every ugly thing
this world can throw at us.
I exist to be only what I already am
nothing more and nothing less
I will not go out in a blaze of glory

I will just be another body
that time forgot.

– CM

Can I just walk off the page?
Can I be an unfinished sentence?
In the middle of the chapter
can I vanish from the story?
So, I don't need to choose
whether to play the hero
and I'm not forced
to be the villain.

I already know how this part goes
so, I'll stop writing now
before the clichés start
before I take up four pages
with my heartfelt monologue.
Can I end this book?
Before it turns to tragedy
can I look fear in the face?
And then slam the cover shut forever?

– CM

I miss the version of me
that wore crop tops and short skirts
just because I liked them.
The version of me
who believed in the saying
'if you've got it, flaunt it.'

I miss the version of me
that showed as much skin as I could
because I was comfortable with it.
The version of me
that never cared if people stared
because I felt untouchable.

I miss the version of me
that wore dresses regularly
because I felt beautiful in them.
The version of me
that wore fishnets and shorts in winter
because I felt powerful.

I miss the version of me
that felt so good in my body
it was almost illegal to feel ashamed.
But, somewhere along my timeline
between then and now
I forgot how I was supposed to bloom.

– CM

I stopped believing
in something that was
bigger than myself
when I discovered that
no one was coming to save me.

I stopped wishing
for something
more than what I am
when I realised that
maybe I wasn't worth saving after all.

I stopped believing in a higher power
because God stood me up
a long time ago
when I fell from my highest
and nobody caught me.

– CM

I'm staying up till 4 am again
but, I'm sleeping most of the day away.
My room is getting messy again
the clothes on the floor are piling up
and I can't tell what's clean or dirty.
I am eating
at least one meal a day.

Haven't I seen this film before?
I think I know how this one goes
but, I guess I'll have to find out
if the ending has changed.
I know I've seen this film
and maybe I already know where this is going
and I want out before the credits roll.

– ***CM***

The voices inside my head
keep acting like they know me
do they really?
Or are they just pretending?
There it goes again
all that deafening silence
it's easy to hear a pin drop
but no one can hear me screaming.

I tried to find solace
within the silence
to find peace
among the voices.

– CM

Suddenly, it got dark
and everything went silent
then for a moment
just a moment
I could finally catch my breath.

The oxygen reached my lungs
and I could feel the air on my skin again
my blood began to flow
my heart started to beat in rhythm
and my mind was finally peaceful.

At that moment
in that single moment
covered in darkness, surrounded by silence
for the first time, in a long time
I could finally feel alive again.

So, when the lights go out
and the silence starts
I'll be begging the stars
and giving everything I have
just so I can feel it again.

– CM

I have lived more lives than I deserve
loved more places than I've seen.
I've fought for the families that I've picked
and cried over thousands of deaths.
I have flown to unimaginable heights
swam to the bottom of oceans.
I have sailed ships to distant lands
and travelled through space and time.
I have fought battles with flaming swords
and used magic for fun.
I have studied in hidden schools
and fallen in love a thousand times.
I have seen worlds end
and watched new ones begin.
I have seen kingdoms fall
and I have seen cities rise.

I have lived thousands of lives
but I intend to live thousands more.
I've had my heart broken more times than I can count
but I intend to let it break again and again.

All because I fell in love with a book
once upon a time.

– ***CM***

The poets often say
your love is
the other half of your soul.
I don't believe that.
My love is not half of anything
she is whole
she is full
and, she is complete.

My love is not half of me
just like I am not half of her
we just happen to be extensions
of each other's hearts.

– CM

To the women who were raised
to not take up space
to never speak too loudly
and to never become a burden.
To the girls who are still being raised
to be seen and not heard
to be polite and kind at all times
to never speak up
and never fight back.

To all of my sisters
all around the world
the ones who are all grown up
and the ones who are still growing.

The world is trying to kill you
I'm sorry, but it's true.
The world is going to continue
to try, and kill you
by taking your voice
and taking your power
and knocking you to the ground.

So, I have one request
just one simple request.
Put your middle finger up
and raise it high
as high as you possibly can
and say it with me.
Fuck it
Fuck that
and most importantly
Fuck them.

– CM

I forgot to think about you today
and I can't figure out if it's bad or good
I can't tell if I should be sad
for not thinking about you
or if I should be happy
because I got to go a day without missing you.

But, if I can forget to remember you
even just for one day
then I am absolutely terrified
that I will forget you completely.

– CM

I have given the best of me
for the good of everyone else.
What am I supposed to do
when I have nothing left to give
when the best of me is long gone
and I'm on my knees praying to be saved
by a God that I don't even believe in
because I'm willing to try anything.

What am I meant to do
when the best parts of me
have disappeared and I'm alone
begging for someone to save me.
When I've wasted the best of who I am
and I'm down on the ground
with dirt on my knees
searching for angels
but I can't fucking find them.

– CM

My pain is my biggest asset
and I have a lot of it.
But, I intend to use every piece of it
I will use my pain for something great
something people won't understand.
I will use my pain to make sure
no one can ever hurt me again.

And, if that makes me a villain
well then, so fucking be it.

– CM

I will be a good victim
and I'll keep all the gory details to myself
and try my best not to traumatise you
while I explain in minimal detail
how I nearly ended.
What I went through
will remain unsaid
like a sickening dark symphony
no one really wants to hear.

I'll be a good victim.
I'll keep it all inside and
keep my nightmares to myself
to protect your fragile mind and heart
from the things you can't handle
and we'll pretend nothing has changed
as I face the darkness alone.

I will be such a good victim
that you won't even know I am one.

– CM

I don't care if you have days
where you need to cry in the shower
or if you have days
when you just can't get out of bed.

As long as you are breathing
you are fighting
and fighting death is not easy.
You are fighting a battle
against a world
that is trying to kill you
and you are winning.

As long as you are breathing
you are winning.

– CM

No one writes about love like this
about the kisses
that make clocks around the world
tick backwards.
About the old souls who
find each other again
and the trembling fingers
on broken and bruised skin.

Nobody writes about love like this
about love that has travelled for 500 years
to reach the two hearts
it's destined for.
Nobody writes about love like ours
love so fragile yet so unbreakable
that our souls have been
forged together for eternity meaning,
we will always find each other in every lifetime.

No one writes about love like ours
so, I will.
I will write about our love
until I run out of words
just to tell you how much
I love you.

I loved you before
in the lives I don't remember.
I love you now
in the life I'm living.
And, if there is life after all of this
I will fight to find you
and I will love you then.

– CM

Death is inevitable.
It is the only promise we have
that is unbreakable.
It is the only promise
we all keep it in the end.

But death holds the promise of peace
that someday, when we've lived our lives
in the wake of our deaths
we will all find each other again.

– CM

We all become stories in the end
that is what life is about.
Everything we have
and everything we are
eventually, becomes
nothing more than
a ghost story.
Shared over drinks
at parties
or around campfires.

– CM

I became besotted with silence
completely and utterly in love
with the idea of being surrounded
by absolutely nothing.
At some point though
I got lonely in the silence
and I choose to look
into the abyss
eventually, the abyss
started staring back.

Until one day, the abyss
turned its back on me.
Even the darkness
of the abyss
needed more than me
it needed more than
I could ever possibly give

How did I manage
to fall in love
with the idea
of absolutely nothing
and to have it
abandon me.

– CM

The greatest lesson
I've ever learnt
came from
a fictional teacher
named Cory Matthews.

And, it is a lesson
I will carry with me
for the rest of my life
and, I will share it
with anyone
willing to listen.

Because he taught me, the secret of life.
'People change people.'
That is life's greatest secret.
What we, do for them.

– CM

There is more to love than
kissing in the rain
more than inside jokes
and cinema dates.

There is more to love than
nightly conversations
more than holding each other
and romance movies.

Love is more than
the things TV shows us
it's more than what
we see in movies
and what we hear
in love songs.

Love can be tragic
and fragile.
It is made up
of broken things
glued back together
in the most beautiful way.

Love can shine
bright enough
to blind you
to everything else

that surrounds you.

– CM

When I was drowning
No one pulled the plug
No one drained the water
there was no life preserver
thrown my way.
No one tried to save me.

So, why should I feel bad
about the fact that
everyone else is burning
and I've got the water
to save them?

Why should I apologise
for not saving them
from burning in fire?
When no one saved me
from drowning in water?

– CM

Everyone has an origin story
you were mine.
But, you didn't make me a hero
you didn't even make me a villain.
You made me a god-damn victim.

Ten years is far too long to remain quiet
to live with your voice
echoing in my head
To have your touch
cling to my skin
to have your scent
clutch at my throat.

For ten-years
I have been a good victim.
I have been a quiet victim
but it is far too long to still get scared
when walking the streets alone.
It is far too long
to still see your face
everywhere I go.

Everyone has an origin story
the one story that makes them
who they really are.
You are my origin story
you made me a victim
but, I refuse to be a quiet one
I refuse to be a good one.

I will scream my story
from the rooftops
and I will tell everyone
who will listen.
I will carve it into stone
and make sure
everyone knows
the monster you are.

– CM

I found too much comfort
in my own mental illness
because honestly
I don’t know what I’d do
without it.
If it suddenly packed its bags
and left me behind
I wouldn’t know how to react.

I found too much comfort
on my down days
and having good days
feels almost foreign
they come far
and few between.

I’m good at being sad
I’m good at being depressed
and I’m good at being lonely.
It’s all I’ve got, sometimes
to a point where
I don’t know who
or what I am
without it all.

– CM

I've always had this feeling of being lonely
for as long as I can remember
but, I've never actually been alone.
I've always been surrounded by people.
Whether it was family
or friends
a boyfriend
or a girlfriend.

In my twenty-five years on this earth
I've never actually been alone
but, I've felt lonely
more times than I can count.

Currently,
there are eight billion plus people
in the world
with more arriving
every minute.
None of us are truly alone
we are always surrounded
either, by loved ones
or by strangers.

I can't help but wonder
how many of us are
truly lonely.
Are you lonely?

– CM

Okay, so maybe
you weren't the love of my life
but you were my love
for that moment.
Perhaps it wasn't true love
and maybe it wasn't forever
I know it wasn't once in a lifetime
but don't you dare say
it wasn't love
because it was.

It was a love story
a tragic
out-of-luck
always meant to end
kind of love story.
It was a different kind of love
a strawberries and cigarettes kind of love
a sweet and bitter kind of love.

You weren't my first love
or my last love
you weren't the love of my life
or the other half of my soul.
You were my love, though
for that time
in that fleeting moment
for those seconds
days, weeks, and months.
I did love you,
I won't ever deny it
or pretend I didn't.
I won't be ashamed of it
because loving you
helped to create
the person I am today.

– CM

Can we just stop everything?
Just for a minute
sixty fucking seconds
that's all I'm asking for.

Sixty seconds
that's all I need.
One minute
for everything to stand still
for the entire world to stop.
Maybe that way,
the voices will stop too
the ones that rattle inside my head
and whisper deafening words
inside my mind.

I just want
sixty fucking seconds
of peace and quiet
one simple minute.

– CM

You have been given the gift
of a broken heart
and as terrible as it is
it is also incredible
that should not be wasted.

Do not take a broken heart
for granted.
Put it to good use
even if you don't know how
put your broken heart to use
and make something
truly extraordinary.
Something you love
or, something you hate
put the broken pieces of your heart
back together
and create something beautiful.

– CM

You will always be
my personal Peter Pan
flying through the stars
forever young
and never growing up.

But, I'll always be
your Wendy Darling
I gave up fairy dust
I forgot how to fly
and I got older.

But, I'll always think of Neverland
and I still dream about
the second star on the right
and flying straight on
till morning.

– CM

The only woman
in a room full of men
struggling to talk over them.
In a room full of men
one feminine voice
trying to be taken seriously
and desperately trying to be heard
that doesn't seem fair, does it?

Why is it so hard for women to be heard?
Why is difficult to be taken seriously?
Because men have no interest
in helping to change the world
that suits them so well.

So, If I get to my feet
and my breathing hitches
and my voice begins to shake
it is not because I don't deserve to be there
it because I am the only woman in that room.

– CM

Can I tell you the truth?
And stop dancing
around my vulnerable heart?
I'll tell you how much I yearn to know you
your skin, your touch, your smell.

I'll tell you all of my vulnerable truths
about how much I wish to drown in you
to be immersed in everything about you
your skin, your blood, your heart.

– ***CM***

I wish I could have loved moderately
just as Friar Laurence advised Romeo
when he told him that
'violent delights have violent endings.'
But, I don't think I have the restraint
or the capacity to love that way
to love anything
or anyone moderately.

I love fiercely,
without remorse, I love fully and unfairly
and I love every piece of me
and with every bit of my heart.
I would burn the world to ash
just to find those that I love
and pull them from the rubble.
I could not love moderately
even if I tried too
I do not know how to follow Friar Laurence's advice.
I cannot love moderately
even though I know
the endings of my stories
will be violent.

– CM

How do we find the strength
and, how do we keep our hearts
while living in a world that is trying to kill us?

We're women, darling. We have to.
Otherwise,
this world will swallow us
whole and devour us
like we are nothing more than tiny mice
rattling around inside the stomach of a beast.

– CM

I sometimes dream
about being fourteen again
and telling your mother
what you did to me
in excruciating detail.

I'd tell her how
you should have stayed in school
because you clearly didn't understand
the meaning of the word 'no'
I'd tell her
how my tears, and begs weren't enough
to stop your wandering hands
as they grabbed at me
like I was meat at a barbecue.
I'd tell her
how you were sweet and kind
at the very beginning
but you turned bitter and cruel
the minute I said no.

I often dream about
being fourteen again
and telling your mother
exactly what kind of man
she raised you to be.
I don't blame her
I don't blame your mother
what do you think would have happened
if I told her in detail
how her darling son was
a cruel and nasty mother-fucker.

Would you have become her greatest shame?
Or, her biggest disappointment?

– CM

Seven years.
A lot can happen
within seven years
for example-

That is how long
it took for NASA to plan and execute
the Apollo 8 Lunar Orbit mission.
It took Alexander the Great
the same amount of time to conquer Persia.
It's the amount of time it took
For Harry Potter to defeat Voldemort.

Between 2012 and 2019 many things took place.
Obama won his second term.
The Higgs Boson was discovered.
Pope Francis was elected.
Liquid water was found on Mars.
The Supreme Court legalised gay marriage.
Chicago Cubs won the World Series.
Donald Trump became President.
TikTok was launched.
The first all-female spacewalk.
Boris Johnson became Prime Minister.
The Avengers saga premiered.

But the best thing that happened
within those seven years
was that, my skin cells regenerated.
So, I finally had skin you'd never touched
cells that didn't remember your fingerprints
or remembered how your hands lingered.

It took seven years, but I finally had a body
that was free from you.

– CM

It was the Bard who once said
'Journeys end in lovers meeting.'
Most of the time
I tend to agree with him
but I can't agree with that.

Some journeys may end in lovers meeting
but, mine did not my journey did not end
when I met my lover
if anything
my journey began there.
It began with meeting her
in being with her
in getting to know her
and in loving her.

So, if I could I
would rewrite the words
and make it say
'Journeys begin in lovers meeting.'

– CM

At five years old, I wanted to spend
the rest of my life being a princess.

At ten years old when I grew up
I wanted to be a vet.

At fifteen years old, I didn't plan for my life
because I wanted to be dead.

At twenty years old, the only thing I wanted
more than anything else was to be loved.

Now, at twenty-five years old
all I really want for my life is to be happy
unconditionally, and irrevocably happy.

– CM

I walk a fine line
between beautifully macabre
and uncharacteristically psychotic
I became a bit of a tragedy
dark, sad, and altogether messy.

I won't be a well-known tragedy
or a story worth telling
the poets will not write about me
or about what I have been through.
They will not call me
a damsel-in-distress or a fighter
they will not compare me
to a warrior or to the gods.
I will never grace the gates
of Valhalla or visit Olympus.
I will not be remembered
as Achilles or Othello are.
My tragedy will not go down in history
as Romeo and Juliet did.

I will not be romanticised
and turned into an iconic heroine
my tragedy and I will disappear.
We will all simply fade away
we will become nothing
but dust and shadows.

– CM

I am a dangerous creature.
Not dangerous as in
violent or volatile
I am dangerous in the way
that I keep my rage behind a smile
and I very rarely smile.
I am dangerous in the way
that I don't necessarily need anyone
or depend on anyone.
In the sense that
I'm not dying to do anything important
and I don't always speak out
or let my emotions take over.

I am a dangerous creature.
I am not dangerous as in
explosive or like a weapon.
I am dangerous in the way
that I am perfectly capable
of staying calm and collected
while walking through hell
with my skin is burning.

– CM

I have spent my entire life
saving everyone else
but who saved me?

No one was there to catch me
while I was falling.
No one threw me a life preserver
while I was drowning at sea.
No one reached for the extinguisher
while I was burning alive.

I have spent so much of my time
saving everyone I care about
but no one even blinked
when I was the one
who needed saving or
when I needed a hero.

– ***CM***

When an intruder breaks into your house
they break windows and locks
things that can be easily fixed.
when an intruder breaks in
they steal things that can be easily replaced.

But, when an intruder breaks into your body
they break bones, promises, and hearts
and what they take cannot be replaced
they take trust, innocence, and your soul.

The intruders are not always strangers
trying to make quick cash
more often than not
they are people you know and trust.

So, when an intruder broke in
all I could do was write poetry
while they were breaking pieces of me.
All I could do was sit quietly in the corner
and wait until they were finished.

– CM

I’ve been told
I have a habit of romanticising things
of trying to find the brightness among things that
have never been touched by the light.
I’ve been told
I have a habit of seeing beautiful things
where there has never been beauty
among the rot and rust.

I’ve tried to find jewels and diamonds
among the ruins and the rubbish
I’ve attempted to find art
in the faded colours and washed-out paints
I’ve listened for a song
when there was no music to begin with.

I’ve been told many times
I have a bad habit of trying
to make life more magical
and more beautiful than it is.

– CM

I like to believe that
Icarus smiled as he fell
as his man-made wings burned
and he fell through the sky.
I also believe that
he would laugh at us
if he knew what we think of him
and that we consider him
a cautionary tragedy.

For one fleeting moment
Icarus had everything
that he ever wanted
right there within reach
right there at his fingertips.
I wouldn't consider that a tragedy.

Icarus may have fallen
but first, at the very least
he flew.
He reached the sun
and sailed through the sky.

Why do we consider him
a cautionary tragedy?
What is more tragic?
Having your dreams at your fingertips
Even just for a moment?
Or never flying at all?
I would choose to fall like Icarus
rather than stay grounded forever.

– CM

Paint me in sunflowers
and cover me in rainbows.
sink me in the meadows
and raise me from the rivers
in which I tried to drown myself.

Surround me with beautiful things
so that I may find
something worth living for.
Show me the wonders of the world
so I can find things
I can look forward to.

Let me look at every piece of art
and allow me to drown in it
play me every kind of music
and let me dance all night.
Surround me with every book
and allow me to fall in love with them
I will watch every film
and live vicariously through them.

Sink me deeply
into everything this word has to offer.

– CM

I may be my father's daughter
that much is true.
But, no one should ever forget
that I am also my mother's child
she gave me my name, and she gave me hers.
My mother gave me everything
that makes me who I am
my voice, my strength, and my spirit.
I am made up of pieces of her
of every spark of magic
that courses through her veins
I am her soul, her heart, and love.

I am many things
but the one I am most proud of is
that I am my mother's child.
I have her capacity for love
and her ability to trust
she showed me how to be strong
and that it's okay to break sometimes

My mother has spent my entire life
showing me love and kindness
tears and smiles.
She has shown me joy and pain
love and loss.
She surrounded me with music
in art and movies and books.
My mother has shown me
everything this world has to offer
and she never once told me
that I couldn't have any of it.

I may be my father's daughter
and I may have his eyes.
but, I am my mothers child all the same
and I have her magic.
That is something far more precious.

– CM

Being a woman means I can do and be many things
but it also means I was born with limitations.

I can be a boss
but, I can't be too bossy.
I can have dreams
as long as I'm realistic about it.
I can be pretty
just as long as I don't tempt anyone.
I can use my voice,
as long as I'm not too loud or heard.
I get to have free will and do what I want
as long as the men say it's okay.

My feminist rants are not about making women strong
women are already strong.
My feminist rants are about change
changing how the world perceives us.

We are women
therefore, we are many things.
We are strong, but we are delicate
we are fragile, but not breakable
we are scared, but we are brave.

In truth, we are many things, but in the end
we are simply women, and we are magic.

– CM

I don’t really know how to be the person
people expect me to be.
I haven’t figured out how to be the daughter
my parents actually deserve.
I haven’t got the hang of being the best kind of friend I can be
and I don’t know how to love someone
without feeling as though I don’t actually deserve them.

I think somewhere along the line
I forgot how to be a person
because I have spent so many years of my life
being nothing more than a problem.

– CM

Have you looked at yourself lately?
Truly looked at yourself?
Have you taken the time to memorise
your face, your body, and the way you move?
Have you noticed how your eyes shine
and the moments they go cold?
Have you taken the time to capture
the curve of your lips?

I think it's about time you did.
I think it's time you noticed
everything pure and beautiful
about yourself.
It's all right there
if you look deep enough
you'll see it, just as I do.

Take the time to look at yourself
to truly see yourself
if the whole world gets to see you
it's only fair that you do too.

– CM

There is a tree outside my bedroom window
and, there's nothing particularly special about it
it's just a tree.

But, there is something about seeing it every day
something about the constant of it
watching the leaves change
and fall
and come back again.
It's simply, just a tree
it's something I see every day
some months it is bare, down to the skeleton
other months it is in full bloom, surrounded by colour

There is a tree outside my bedroom window
there is nothing special about it
it's just a tree
but it is more constant than the sun
more constant than rain or snow.
It is there when I sleep and when I wake
it is there when I smile and when I cry.

There is a tree outside my bedroom window
and I watch it blow in the wind
as though it is performing a dance
only it knows.
There is a tree outside my bedroom window
and it's just a tree
but is also hope, hope for tomorrow
because I know it will be there
and a promise, a promise for change
because it is constantly changing.

– CM

I loved you.
In happiness
in sadness
and when it hurt so much
it felt like I might die.
I loved you.

I loved you.
Beyond doubt
beyond hope
and beyond all logical reason.
I loved you.

I loved you.
When my mind screamed no
when my heart couldn't take it
and when I couldn't understand why.
I loved you.

I loved you.
But the most shocking part was
you had the audacity to love me back
beyond everything.
You loved me.

I loved you.
Beyond everything I am
and in spite of everything
I've been through
and most importantly
I loved you on purpose
and I will continue to do so
for the rest of my life.

I love you
I loved you.

– CM

It’s hidden in an old song
you thought you’d forgotten
it’s in the scenes of a movie
the one you haven’t watched since childhood
it’s in the rainy days under blankets
and the snow days with hot chocolate
it’s the secret kept in your childhood diary
Christmas mornings and Sunday dinners.

It’s in your mum’s cooking
and, your siblings laugh
the childhood piggyback rides from your dad
it’s in a hug from your grandmother
and your cousins smile
the way your uncle ruffles your hair
and the cups of tea your aunt makes.

It is home.
It’s being safe again
all the familiar smells and sounds
its heartbeats and smiles.
Home is the history, the present, and the future
coming together in a neat bow.

It’s home.

– CM

Nothing ever ends poetically
things end,
And we create poetry
from those endings.

We're human.
It is in our nature
to make beautiful things
out of the painful endings
we all experience.

We have been raised on
once upon a time, and
wishing on stars
we grew up believing in
happily ever after, and
fairytale endings.

We are human.
It is in our nature
to hope for happy endings
beautiful endings
poetic endings.

– CM

A pedestal made from broken bones,
and sharpened glass
is still the pedestal I am placed on.

A crown forged from
barbed wire, and rose thorns
is still the crown impaled on my head.

A kingdom built up from
poisoned blood, and raging hellfire
is still the kingdom I am forced to rule.

A pedestal, a crown, and a kingdom

The life of a damned ruler
the life of a cursed queen.

– CM

I would have turned around
and not look back
if I knew then
what I know now.

I hardly knew anything
but, some days
I thought I knew far too much
I thought I knew everything.

– CM

I am a lot of things to a lot of people.
I am my parents' daughter
my brothers' little sister.
I am a niece and a granddaughter
I am a fiancé and a friend.
But, before I belong to anyone else
I am my own person
I belong to myself.

– ***CM***

I appear to be destined
to only write sad poems
and letters I'll never send.

Perhaps, I write poems
because my sadness is
the only thing I can explain
and it's the only feeling
that I know how to handle.

Maybe, I never sent those letters
because to me
my words are like diamonds
and no one ever gives away
a diamond for free.

– ***CM***

I think I was born broken
a little bit twisted, with a chip on my shoulder
maybe it's my personal curse
to simply, grin and bear it.
I think some people are born content
specifically, born to be happy
some people were simply
born to be alive.

I think I was born broken.
Some people are born to be alive
I was born to be broken.

– CM

I will never be the woman people write stories,
or poems, or songs about
I will never be the focus of a love song,
or a name in a sonnet, or a damsel in a story.

I will never be that woman.

– CM

I have monsters rattling around inside my head
constantly screaming for attention
trying their hardest to claw their way to the surface
it's only when they quiet down
that I can finally feel free
and that I can actually step out of the darkness.

I may not shine in the sunlight but,
at least when I'm out there
my monsters are pushed into the shadows
and I don't have to hear them, or even see them.
When I step out of the darkness and into the sunlight
I can pretend my monsters aren't monsters at all.

– CM

I have spent my days trying to make myself smaller
to fit into the boxes of what I should be
the perfect daughter, the perfect sister
perfect friend, and the perfect girl.
I am constantly trying to fit into those tiny boxes.
So, I tried my hardest, every day
to make everything about myself smaller
my voice, my thoughts my body, and my moods.

I am a big person, I have always been a big person
so I spend years, months, weeks, and days
trying to make myself less like me
that way, there would be less of me.

– CM

I hold my rage inside of me
to the point where it spills out
in unstoppable, hysterical tears
that people will refer to as
'female rage'
because it can't just be rage
it has to be a female
because only women cry with rage
right?

I hold my rage inside of me
to the point where it spills
out in unstoppable, hysterical tears
not because I am a woman
but, because if I let that rage out
even for one single minute
I won't be able to pull it back
if I let that rage out
I will have no control over it.

– CM

The bumps in the road we're travelling
often, turn into mountains
but at least the view is always
Beautiful

– CM

I’ve loved a lot
I’ve loved people who didn’t deserve it
people who didn’t want it, and
people who would never love me back.
I’ve loved a lot and each, and every time
it was a wonderful experience
because at least I got to love
it was better than nothing.

*– **CM***

I think I'm pretty damaged
I think I'm beyond repair
that I'll never truly be fixed.
I used to believe that someday
I'd just wake up, and be whole again
but, I guess it isn't that easy.

– CM

I often find it hard to accept endings
to accept that something is truly over
even though every ending is
meant to be a new beginning.

I still tend to avoid them
if I can.

*– **CM***

Can I come home someday?
Not to the place made of walls and windows
but home, the place where I belong
where my heart and soul live.

Can I come home again?
Even if I'm still lost?

– CM

I cried the first time I had *sex*
not during, but after
once I was home, and alone
it wasn't like I hadn't planned it,
for that day, at that time, with that person
I don't know why, I just did.

The first time I had *sex*
I cried after, in the shower
as I scrubbed at my skin
as though, maybe if I was clean enough
I could undo it, I could take it back.

– CM

I made it through the year again
even though with every month
everything continued to get harder.
but, I made it.

I made it to November again.

– CM

I'm not afraid of the dark any more
at one point, I think I used to be
I think I used to be so scared
sleeping alone was my worst nightmare.

I'm not afraid of the dark any more
if anything, I'm besotted with it.

– CM

The ghosts of who I am
who I was, and
who I desperately want to be
cling to me, and follow me around
as though I am meant
to lead them somewhere
but, I don’t know where.

My ghosts haunt me
all day, every day
they watch me go through life
as if, I am their new
favourite show.

– CM

The truth is:
I could change everything
about myself
from my hair and clothes
to my thoughts and beliefs
and, I would still never be enough.

<u>I would never be good enough.</u>

– CM

I have spent my entire life
pulling my punches
biting my tongue
sitting on my hands
and zipping my lips.
I have spent my entire life
with both my hands
tied behind my back.

What happens when I'm finally free
of everything holding me back?
What do you think will happen
when I finally stop pulling my punches?

– CM

So, if I'm being honest
maybe I don't speak up enough
I keep all my secrets to myself
and close to my chest.
I keep pieces of myself
wrapped up so tightly
some have never seen
the daylight
Some of them never will.
There are parts of me
that I have kept hidden
for so long
even I wouldn't recognise them.

– CM

I don't think I should be
mad at myself
for feeling everything
that I choose to feel
or, for leaving my heart open
to the idea of feeling everything.

I don't think I should be
mad at myself for that
and, I should never
be made to apologise for it.

– ***CM***

I would consider myself
a hoarder
but, I don't hoard objects
I hoard pain and trauma.
I cling to it wrapping my fingers around it
as though it is my only lifeline.

I cling to pain and trauma
because it fuels me
more than satisfaction, or joy.
I hoard pain and trauma
because it keeps me alive.

– ***CM***

If boys will be boys
and men will be men
then it's only fair
that women shall be women
and we will do what we do best
we will talk.

We will talk until
the truth flows through the streets
like a river flows to the ocean
unstoppable and unyielding.
We will talk until
the truth of who you are
is carved in stone
and going down in history.

If boys will be boys
and men will be men
then women will be women
and we will talk
and we will ruin you
with nothing but our voices.

– CM

I never grieved
for the pieces of myself
that I lost to trauma
I just smiled and moved on.
I never said goodbye
to the girl I was
or the one I wanted to be
I just flipped my hair
and walked away.

I never grieved or said goodbye
to the things I was leaving behind
the parts of me I was losing
I never cried for them
there are no headstones
or statues for me to visit
there are no anniversaries
for me to remember.

Those parts of me
that girl I could have been
the future I could have had
it's just dust and shadows now.

– CM

They never actually burnt, drowned
or tortured witches
they burnt, drowned, and tortured women
innocent women that they feared.
Women who simply had the nerve
to want more than what they had
and speak up for what they wanted.
Men caused the mass hysteria
yet, it was the women
who paid the price

How long will it be before history repeats?
How long before it happens again?
What happens if the hysteria wins?

They tried to burn us once
They will try again.

– CM

Women make up
51% of the population
yet, we still take up less space
than we deserve.

51% of the population.
That is the majority vote
yet, we don't have as much
space, say, rights, or even time
as we should.

51% of the population.
That is the majority of the noise
yet, we have no voices.
Correction, we do have voices
we have simply been silenced.

Women are the majority
women have more power and
have more votes than any man.
It is time we started acting like it.

– CM

Don’t just sit there
and act well-behaved.
Get up
lift your chin
and, fucking scream
scream until someone hears you
until someone listens.

– CM

Pretty boys don't always stay pretty
well, maybe on the outside they do
but, I've known a lot of pretty boys.
It's like they have a candy-coating
all sugary, sticky, and sweet
but once you crack it open
the pretty is just gone
what you find underneath is
dark, twisted, and messy.
Pretty boys don't always stay pretty
no matter how much
you want them too.

Pretty boys don't stay pretty forever.

– CM

I always thought
writing would be easier
with a fresh broken heart
than with my old memories
but, my brain seems to be stuck,
stuck in a state of unknowing, and
unmoving.

I always thought
fresh heartbreak
would be easier
to write about
but, if anything
it's harder
having everything frozen in place.

– CM

When it comes to my writing
I've decided to follow the
Taylor Swift rule:

If you don't want me to write about you then don't do bad things.

– CM

I have been dragged
down to depths
that I didn't know existed
by monsters, I didn't know I had
but you, you were
the saving-grace
I didn't know I needed.

But, even saving-graces
can't save those
who won't allow themselves
To be saved.

– ***CM***

You are gone, but
you are everywhere
I know exactly where to find you.
You are in the sunset
and in every wave in every ocean
you are in every grain of sand
on every beach.
You are in every winter chill
and, every summer breeze
in every raindrop
And, every inch of sunshine.
You are in the trees
and in every flower.

You are gone
but, you are everywhere
and hidden in everything.

– CM

I want love
beautiful TV show love
Stiles and Lydia
Monica and Chandler
Tara and Willow
kind of love.

I want love
magical movie love
Tony and Pepper
Morticia and Gomez
Will and Elizabeth
kind of love.

I want love
insatiable book love
Harry and Ginny
Magnus and Alec
Kate and Anthony
kind of love.

I want love
beautiful
magical
insatiable
love.

– CM

My family tree
is constructed of
slightly broken and bent branches
which belong to
slightly broken and bent people.

My family tree
has been standing
for so many years
and we will continue
to stay standing
for many years to come.

We may be broken and bent
but, we do not waver
we do not shake, and
we do not fall.
My family tree is still standing
we are still standing.

So, we're good,
yeah, still good.

– CM

I always thought that
I was so lucky because
somehow I had fooled people
into thinking
I was so lovable that
they fell in love with me.

I always thought that
I was lucky because
people had fallen in love
with the image of me
I so wanted the world to see.

I thought I was lucky
but, I was the furthest thing
from it.

And now, I'm not sure
if I ever truly was loved
or, if maybe
I just loved them so much
that I convinced myself
they loved me too.

– CM

A small-town girl
with small-town dreams.

A small-town witch
with big universe magic.

– CM

'The only natural resource that the world has too much of...Girls.'
—Dreykov, Black Widow

Girls.
Women.

Apparently, the world has
far too many of us
and we are expendable.

We take up too much space
we make too much noise
and we do too much.
We are the one thing
the world has too much of
and instead of rejoicing
in female solidarity
we are made to feel
ashamed of it.

As if being surrounded
by girls and women
is a truly terrible thing

– CM

'Just another beast to kill.'

How redundant,
for men to say that
about a woman
but, Medusa
was never a beast
or a monster.

Medusa was a victim
an ignored, neglected
and betrayed victim.

I am an advocate for Medusa.

– CM

Women are always underestimated.
we are always perceived as weak
yet, for generations
we have bled, and been burned
we have been broken and bent
for generations
we have been forged
in flames and torment.
We may be fragile
but we are not weak
we are not lost in the fire
we are built from the flames.

– CM

I would stay if only
you'd give me
a reason to hang on.

I would stick around
if only I could
find something
to hold on to.

I would be there
if only I could
convince myself
you still need me.

But, I would leave
if you asked me
to leave you
behind.

– ***CM***

So, if I'm honest.

If you knew the extent
of what I've been through
you wouldn't question
the lengths I go to
protect myself
from everyone
and everything in this world.

If you knew the true extent
of the damage
that has been done to me
you would understand
why I wrap myself up
in my very own mind
and my very own worlds.

– CM

Sometimes
endings don’t bring
new beginnings.
Sometimes
endings are simply
just endings.

The clock stops ticking
the carousel stops spinning
and, the music stops playing.

Sometimes
endings are just endings
there is no great logic
no new beginning
and no moral to the story.

Everything just stops
and, the end is just
the end

– CM

I’ve perfected the art
of being alone
and, being lonely
if anything,
I thrive in it.
I am wonderful
at being alone.

I wake up alone
when the sun rises
I go to sleep alone
when the moon
comes up.
I sing alone in my rooms
I write alone, always
and, I thrive alone

I am perfectly
good at being alone
I just don’t like it
very much.

– CM

Broken people have a tendency
to remain broken long after
we are glued back together.
We're never really, fixed
not completely, anyway.

There is no fixing us
we are glued, and taped together
but, those wounds
can always reopen.

– CM

No one truly knows
just how much a heart can handle
how much pain, or love
loss, or joy
a human heart can hold.

No one has measured it
not doctors, or nurses
poets, or musicians
authors, or artists
there is no one in the world
who knows the true amount
our hearts can take.

We just accept everything
and, we hope for the best
we take it into our hearts
and, we hope our hearts can take it.

– CM

I'm still young
and, I'm still learning.
I have a lot left to learn
and, as much as I pretend I'm not
I'm still naive.

I believe that I am safe
that I am protected
I convince myself
the storm won't touch me
and the darkness
cannot reach me
even though
it already has.

My naivety is like
the sword of Damocles
hanging over my head
and I am patiently waiting
for the sword to fall
and for my execution.

– CM

Be gentle with me, please
I'm still adjusting
I'm still recovering
and, I'm still adapting
to a world where
I'm clean.
I'm still learning
how to cope in a world where
I'm not cutting myself open
just to feel alive.

Be gentle with me, please.
I'm still learning how to be okay.

– CM

I have a scarlet letter
engraved on my chest
because of you.
Bright, bloody, and raw
for the whole world to see
and you'll never understand
what that feels like.

I wish I could take from you
even just half
of what you took from me.
But, you'll never understand
how it feels to be branded
because of something
someone else chose to do.

I got a scarlet letter
because of you.

– CM

To whom do I owe the biggest apology?

Myself or
the people who love me?

I think I owe it to myself
no one has given up on me
the way I have given up on myself
and no one betrays me
like I do.

I am my own worst enemy.

– CM

I don't think I ever learnt
how to love fully
or how to love properly.

When I had it
I don't think I said it enough
actually, I know I didn't
and, I know I didn't show it.

So, I'll nurse my broken heart
put all the pieces back in place
and, try to fix what's broken.

But, who will love me
when I can't love them back.

– CM

I remain unfinished
I am not complete
and, I remain half-done.

I have not lived a life yet
not one worth sharing
I have not lived yet
so this cannot be my life.

I cannot continue to live
while unfinished.

– CM

Maybe, I am
by definition, unlovable
or at least, not lovable for long.

No one wants to love someone
who cannot love them back
the way they deserve.

I am, by definition
unlovable.

– CM

You have a heartless kind of magic
the magic forged under an eclipse
in the hands of someone
who does not deserve it.

Your magic does not bring beauty
it does not bring hope or eternal bliss
it does not bring balance.
Your magic does not walk the line
between good and evil
life and death
light and dark.

You have heartless magic
that was forged beyond the line
and held by people
who do not deserve it.

– CM

My mind is a labyrinth
but there is no Goblin King
or riddle asking doorknobs.
There is no worm shouting 'ello
or Ludo to befriend.

I am stuck in an inescapable maze
built from my very own trauma, and pain
I constructed the labyrinth to avoid my pain
yet, I am constantly stuck inside of it.

My mind is a labyrinth
but not the fun kind that comes
with singing, dancing, and friends
and, I don't get to go home in the end.

– CM

I would have loved you
until the end of time
until the clocks stopped ticking
and forever ran out.

I may not have shown it
in all the right ways
or, said it enough
but please, know this.

I would have loved you
in my very own way
and, in the best way
I could offer you
until forever ran out of time.

I would have loved you
forever and always.

– CM

I think I'm allowed to forgive myself
for leaving pieces of who I am
scattered throughout time.
I think I'm allowed to forgive that.

I think I'm allowed to forget about those parts
the parts I left behind
all the broken pieces of me
that slipped away into nothing.
I'm allowed to forget about them.

– CM

I wish I hadn't given up
my *girlhood* so easily.

That I hadn't wished away
my childhood that was built on
scraped knees, muddy footprints
Barbie dolls, and water balloon fights.
That I hadn't outgrown
my teenage years filled with
first crushes, stolen kisses
movie nights, and finding myself.

I wish I hadn't given up
my *girlhood* so easily
by growing up so quickly
and losing pieces of myself
before I knew who I was.

I wish I hadn't given up
my *girlhood* so easily.

That I hadn't crossed my legs
when they told me to
sit like a lady.
That I hadn't closed my mouth
when they told me, I was being
far too loud.
That I hadn't stopped
jumping in puddles, and
making my Barbies kiss.

I wish I hadn't given
up my *girlhood* so easily.

– CM

I am the girl, that was never enough,
the one who just wanted a bit more love
I am the girl you forgot when you learnt her name
and the one who was never going to be *'the one.'*

I am the girl whose kisses you got sick of
when you learnt the shape of her lips
the one who wanted the white dress
I am the girl who wanted the fairytale ending
and the one who was never going to get it.

– CM

I am yours, but
you are not mine.
You haven’t been mine
for a very long, but
I am still waiting
for you to come back
to decide you want me once more
and that you love me again.

I am yours, always.
But, you are not mine
not anymore.

– ***CM***

I’ve known heartbreak before
and I’ve felt it more than once
so, I guess you could say
we are, somewhat, acquainted
almost, kind of, friends.
When heartbreak comes to me
it crawls out of the shadows
and curls itself around me
like an unwanted, ghostly hug
consuming my body entirely
until I am nothing
but, heartbreak and shadows.

Heartbreak is a dear friend of mine.
The one that never wants to leave.

– CM

I wish I could bloom
into something bright
and something beautiful
that I could become
a natural masterpiece,
I wish I could bloom
into something magnificent
and entirely glorious
but, maybe all that I am
is all that I was destined to be.

But still, I wish I could bloom.

– CM

Today is the beginning of the end.
the sun is finally setting
the curtain call has come
and it's time for me to take
my final bow.
But, this is just the beginning
of saying goodbye, and letting go
the beginning of the pain
I've always tried to outrun, and
the ending I always knew was coming.

Today, today is the beginning of the end
so, I will take my final bow
and greet the end like an old friend.

– ***CM***

Just because we're broken
doesn't mean we deserve to be lonely.
I wish there was a place
where all the broken people
could go to be together,
a place where we didn't
have to hide the broken
pieces of ourselves
just to live our lives.

I wish there was a place
where all the broken people
could go to be together.

– CM

There is something heart-warming
about hugging my younger cousins
wrapping them in my arms
and holding on to them so tightly.
I have watched them out-grow everything
their toys, their clothes, and my arms
but, eventually, they come back again.

There is something so heart-warming
about my hugging my younger cousins
after I have watched them outgrown me
and watched them come back again.

– CM

I want you to think about me
and remember everything
remember me, and us
every word we shared
each moment we lived.
I want you to remember
the way we used to love
and, the memories we made.

I want you to think about me
and everything we shared.

– ***CM***

One day,
I'll be able to tell
the difference between
love, in love, and loved.

One day,
I'll find a way
to understand exactly how
we went from being
platonic love, to being in love
to having loved each other once.

One day,
I'll be able to
figure it all out
and I'll find a way
not blame myself
for losing love.

– CM

I used to believe that
my wretched little heart
was the most unlovable
thing about me
until you came along
and fell in love with me
not despite it, but because of
my wretched little heart.

If I didn't have
such a wretched little heart
would you have really
loved me to begin with?

– CM

Do not be deceived
by my pretty little words
and my delicate sentences.
The things I have to say
are not always considered
so beautiful.

I have a bad habit
of wrapping horrible stories up
in beautiful paragraphs
because I have somehow
perfected the art of
turning horrible truths
into pretty little lies.

Do not be deceived
by my pretty little words
and my delicate sentences.
I wrap my darkness up
in perfect pretty words
so that people don't try
to look too close.

– CM

I am a child of Aphrodite
wrapped in beauty and love.

I am a child of Hecate
with magic crackling in my veins and fingertips.

I am a child of Athena
with a mind that is wise and logical.

I am a child of Nyx
with a soul that is devoted to night.

I am a child of Artemis
with a spirit that is free and wild.

I am a child of Hebe
with a heart that is forever young, and youthful.

I am a child of Nike
with a lifetime spent surrounded by art and music.

I am a child of Olympus
I am gifted, I am glorious, I am magic.

– ***CM***

Loving me shouldn't be hard
it shouldn't be a challenge
you need to accept
or, a game you can win
loving me shouldn't be hard.

I don't know why
I can't make people
love me or why
I can't find a way to
make them stay with me.
I don't know why
people run away from me
and take their love with them.

Loving me shouldn't be hard.
Loving me shouldn't be difficult.

– CM

I fucked a narcissist once
and, I really wouldn't recommend it.
He didn't love me
or even really like me
he liked how I made him feel
and the noises I faked just for him.

I fucked a narcissist once
or, maybe it was twice.
I didn't really like it
but we gave each other
what we wanted.
An ego boost for him
and self-hatred for me.

I fucked a narcissist once
I wouldn't recommend it.

– ***CM***

And, so I take my pills
just like the doctor said
and I sleep, and I dream
and hope nothing changes
but I pray everything does
again, and again, and again.

And, so I take my pills
I read my books
sing my songs, and
recite my oaths
then I go to bed
and toss and turn
then do it all again.

And, so I take my pills
and I carry on
Because it's all I know
how to do.

– ***CM***

Being a poet is a dangerous thing
we bare our souls
for the world to see
and we drip words like blood
pouring from our veins.
We tear ourselves apart
so others can read and analyse
and we spill all our stories
and our deepest secrets
onto pages for people we don’t know
to read and relate to.

– ***CM***

In this world
we must bleed
in order to grow.
We must pay in blood
to simply exist in this world.

I paid in blood to be here.
I paid in blood to survive.

– CM

Love notes and ghost stories
are made up of the same things
they are beautiful and broken
miserable and lovely
forgotten and unforgettable
all at the same time.

Love notes and ghost stories
are made up of the same things.

– CM

All my future loves
will know your name.

Will yours know mine?

– CM

You are my almost.
We were almost forever
and almost always
we almost made it
to the end of the line.
You are now and
for as long as I live
you will always be
my almost.

– CM

I was born from dragon fire and magic
created from stardust and wishes.
Though I am made of
blood, bone, and flesh
I come from so much more
from hundreds of years worth of
art, and memories, and stars, and music
I come from generations of
all the magical things in this world.

– CM

I am not a poet
I am a woman.
A woman who feels
an unnatural amount
who feels too much at once
and who has too little knowledge
of how to cope with those feelings.

I am not a poet
I am woman
and I make no excuses
for how I feel.

– CM

I am a feminist
but I am exhausted being a woman.

I am exhausted from having
to scream just to be heard
from having all of my anger
reduced down to 'hysterics'
of being groped, and
cat-called, and sexualised
since I was thirteen.
I am sick and I am exhausted
of being seen as property
and not as a person
of being complimented and
insulted all in one sentence
from having my entire gender
reduced to less than what we are.

I am a feminist
But I am exhausted being a woman.

– *CM*

I was born to fall
madly in love with ghosts
to only love the ones
who would never, and
could never love me back.
I was made to dance
softly and silently with ghosts
to glide through empty hallways
to the echo of an old song
one that ended long ago
with someone whose touch
I will never feel.

I was born to love ghosts
and only ghosts.

– CM

What if I go crazy again?
then what happens?
What if I suddenly lose it again
and this time
I don’t get better?
What if this time
I just stay lost and crazy
forever.

– CM

To some people, I am a blessing
To others, I am a curse.
I am annoying, tolerable, kind, and a bitch.
I am too much, too little, too quiet, and too loud.
Likewise, I am shy, anxious, too sad, too happy, too feminine, and not feminine enough.
I am too honest, too much of a liar, too fake, and too real.

To some, I am a curse, to others I am a blessing.
I am sweet, vindictive, family, a stranger, a friend, and an enemy.
I am everything, to everyone, at all times
but, no one cares what I am to myself.

– CM

Oh, my darling
loving you was thrilling
but, terrifying at the same time
to be so in love with you
my world cracked in two
when you left,
Oh, my darling
It was terrifyingly, thrilling
to love you.

– CM

I want to write a love letter
to every woman, I've ever known
and make sure they know
just how magnificent they are
to tell them how much
they are adored and loved.

I want to write a love letter
to every woman, I've ever known
so that I can tell them
all the things they need to hear
to tell them they are glorious
and beautiful, and divine.

I want to write a love letter
to every woman, for every woman.

– CM

It took me a long time
to realise that having sex
did not determine my worth.
Just because I was doing it
didn't mean I was loved
or, even wanted.

– CM

I know that we are
coming from different directions
but, maybe we can find a way
to meet in the middle
to find some common ground.

– CM

I'll keep waiting until
you want me again
for you to come back
and tell me
you changed your mind
that you want
all of me again.

So, I'll keep waiting
with my whole life
on hold
until you come running
back to me again.

– CM

Does she know how
I pray to the old gods
and whisper secret wishes
to the universe
for just one more hour?

Does she know that
my fingertips flutter
over the blurred edges
of my favourite memories
just to feel her skin again?

Does she know how
I cling to those songs
we once sang along too
just so I can live
those moments again?

Does she know that
everything about her
still surrounds me
like dust collecting
in a mausoleum?

– CM

Someday…
Someday, I'll be pretty
not pretty to you
but pretty to me.

I will be so pretty
I will smile, constantly
and only cry happy tears
in front of the mirror.

Oh, someday
someday I will be pretty
pretty to me.

– CM